Nicola Happé has been a chiro
her own clinic in 2016. Prior to this, she worked in various
roles within administration and sales. Nicola lives in
Boumemouth with no pets, as the two grown up children she
has have been enough. Her favourite thing to do is to see live
music whether that is in a local pub, gig venue or at a festival.
'A Happé Ending' is Nicola's first book but may not be her
last!

To Dylan and Molly for making me look like a good parent.

Nicola Happé

A HAPPÉ ENDING

AUSTIN MACAULEY PUBLISHERS™

LONDON • CAMBRIDGE • NEW YORK • SHARJAH

A CIP catalogue record for this title is available from the British Library.

ISBN 9781528984218 (Paperback)
ISBN 9781528984225 (ePub e-book)

www.austinmacauley.com

First Published (2020)
Austin Macauley Publishers Ltd
25 Canada Square
Canary Wharf
London
E14 5LQ

Thank you to Ruth Sturdy for getting me through it with our constant chats about Pete.

Thank you to Hannah Turner for your ears and your well needed encouragement throughout the writing of this book.

Thank you to Rosie Durant; without you, the book would have taken a lot longer to publish.

A massive thank you to all my friends and family.

Chapter One

Death, demise, passing, expiration, the end, loss of life, final exit, six feet under, fall off the perch, eternal rest, deceased, ride the pale horse, kick the bucket, kick the calendar, expired, counting worms, informal snuffing, termination, the cure for life, bite the dust, take a last bow, take a dirt nap, brown bread, go belly up, gone to a better place, turning the lights out, pull the curtains, join the great majority, cark it, end of the line, judgment day, push up daisies, assume room temperature, check out, to shuffle off this mortal coil. Basically and unsurprisingly, at some point, this is an unavoidable event that will happen to us all.

I never really had any dealings with death until I was 25 years old, when my oldest grandparent died. All my grandparents had good innings, thankfully, so it was relatively easy to celebrate their lives when they'd gone. The first grandparent I lost was my mum's dad; he was 92 years old and had been living in a nursing home for a few years prior, so it was kind of a relief when he finally let go. His funeral is one that I will never forget, and not just because it popped my funeral virginity.

The day of the funeral was lovely and sunny, and the service was a cremation. My mum, being one of eight kids, had quite a large, widespread family so the ones that could, travelled from afar to be there. My mum was the child that had stayed; living close to her parents, therefore ultimately becoming their carer, so we didn't have far to travel that day. My Welsh uncle, auntie and two cousins, unfortunately, got the time of the funeral wrong, but they did have a lovely picnic in the forest and arrived at the crematorium for the correct time of a complete stranger's funeral instead. The wake was held at my grandma's bungalow and was a chance for the family to catch up, including the Welsh ones.

My mum's youngest brother, my uncle Peter, has Down's syndrome, and one of the things he loves doing—apart from teasing people, collecting deodorant and dusting empty bottles—is watching soap operas on television. At this point, in the afternoon of the funeral, he was sat inside, happily watching *Neighbours* with Trish, his carer. A lovely and peaceful afternoon was being had, sitting outside soaking up some sunshine in the garden whilst looking at old photos and reminiscing. Trish then wondered outside and asked my sister—who is an air stewardess—when she was next due to fly to New York.

"This Thursday," came my sister's response.

"Hmmm, I don't think you'll be going!" Trish replied as she beckoned us to follow her into the lounge.

In the lounge, we found a slightly annoyed Peter, still sat in front of the television, but he was complaining that his programme had gone off and that a helicopter had hit a building. *Neighbours* had indeed been replaced by a news flash, but Uncle Peter had got his flying machines mixed up. The date was 11th September 2001, and we were all watching the television, as the second plane hit the south Twin Tower building in New York.

In the years following, a couple more grandparents at ripe old ages fell off their perches and thankfully, their funerals didn't share a date with any other dramatic events. It was unusual and relieving that at the age of 31, I hadn't lost anyone around me suddenly and unexpectedly. My husband and I even had a conversation one evening about how weird it was that a group of friends as diverse and crazy as ours hadn't suffered any casualties of life to date. Conversations were never dull in our house, which brings me neatly onto the subject of my husband, Pete.

Some Pete facts for you:

Peter James Happé was born on 6th July 1976.

He was born in Tidworth Military Hospital in Tidworth, Wiltshire.

His younger sister was born 14 months later on 6th September 1977.

Moved around various military bases for the first three years of his life.

Lived in Cyprus from the age of four until six, when he moved to Bournemouth.

His mother, a devout Catholic, was a nurse.

His father, an army personnel, was a chronic adulterer.

His first job was a paper round.

He went to Corpus Christi Roman Catholic Primary School in Pokesdown.

He went to St Peters Roman Catholic Secondary School and continued onto sixth form there.

During this time, he worked part time in a local café.

He went to Leicester De Monfort University and studied marine biology.

He dropped out of university after six months of studying.

He worked in a betting shop then at a café in Tesco before getting a job working down the beach, which he did for a few years.

Then he worked in a mobile phone shop before studying part time to become an electrician.

He had worms at the age of eight.

His appendix burst and had to be removed at the age of 13.

On the way back from a school trip at the age of 15, he drank a whole bottle of whisky and subsequently had to have his stomach pumped.

He loved skateboarding and surfing.

He had a tramp stamp tattoo, which was shit; another tattoo down his left torso and one down his left arm. Both of those were good.

He had his left nipple, tummy and tongue pierced.

He later lost his left nipple piercing along with half of his left nipple in a skateboarding accident.

He nearly died whilst surfing in Indonesia when he fell off his board, lost both contact lenses and got caught in the washing machine of waves.

He drank a whole bottle of whisky all to himself in the hour after this near-death experience.

Whilst travelling, he got called 'Jesus' by some Indonesian locals, due to his long hair and blue eyes.

He was a grumpy old man in a young person's body.

He had a quick and very dark sense of humour.

He was very clumsy.

He loved drinking alcohol.

He LOVED drinking alcohol.

He didn't have an off-switch when partaking in that activity.

During a rainy morning whilst in Bali, he got bored, cut his own hair and gave himself a fringe.

His hair started going grey at the age of 19.

Sat in a bin at one Glastonbury festival, saying hello to the passersby.

Got lost at V festival for the whole day after a game of playing 'where's wally' and miraculously found everyone as we were just getting into the van to come home.

When working down the beach with a hangover, a friend/colleague took Pete's easy shift working the cliff lift, meaning Pete had to do the hard work. Pete was not happy about this, so he wrote the word CUNT in very large letters in the sand so the friend/colleague could see it during the whole of his shift.

Chapter Two

I met Pete when he and I were both 21 years old, in our local drinking establishment, Bar Max. I actually met his sister Ruth first, in said drinking establishment, when she was with an old friend of mine, who I had bumped into in the toilets like you do. It turned out to be a moderate drinking session with lots and lots of giggles that night and I knew I'd made a new friend in Ruth.

A couple more pub trips later over the next week or so (I lived quite close to this pub), and I had been introduced to Pete, briefly. I thought he was pretty cool and good-looking; he had just come back from travelling and was totally my type, visually. So, during an afternoon drinking session with the mate I was with when I first met Ruth, we happened to notice Pete walk in and sit at a table over the other side of the bar. He was sat on his own briefly, whilst his mate was getting their pints in. As we sat there, gazing at this lonely, handsome, longhaired surfer dude, he happened to lift his t-shirt up to scratch his tummy and revealed a slightly rotund belly. Being somewhat disappointed that a six-pack wasn't revealed, we decided not to let that put us off completely and invited him and his mate over to join us for a drink at our table anyway.

Thankfully, they accepted our invitation and joined us, and the conversation flowed, as they say. Pete's mate was actually Ruth's boyfriend at the time, so it was nice to meet him and the both of them definitely made us laugh a lot that afternoon. Pete's current job was a 'deckie' otherwise known as a deckchair attendant down the beach, which made me fancy him even more. We seemed to have the same interests, taste in music, lifestyle choices and even had some mutual friend connections, bizarrely. I really enjoyed his company

13

and wanted to see him more, but didn't want to seem too keen, therefore, we had a few unplanned spontaneous meet ups over the following week or so, obviously in that same pub.

After one late night drinking session, we found ourselves being kicked out at closing time. We certainly weren't ready to call it a night yet and due to the proximity of the pub to my home, I used the best chat-up line I could think of. I invited Pete back to my flat for a smoke. I think his eyes actually lit up when I mentioned I had some green, so he quickly took me up on my offer and we started dating.

After about six months of going out together, I fell pregnant. Whoopsy! Totally not planned for and a slightly frightening situation to find ourselves in at the age of 22. And again at the age of 25, although the second time round wasn't quite as daunting as the first time. As neither of my kids were planned, I call them happy accidents. And due to the fact that they left me feeling like a zombie through lack of sleep and a general slave, I don't think there would have ever been a time in my life when I would have chosen that.

So, after birthing the kids, the marriage occurred. I say 'marriage' and not 'wedding' as it was really just a name-changing formality so I would share the same surname as my children. Pete had 'proposed' or rather, asked me if I wanted the ring that he was presenting to me, whilst I was in labour with Dylan, walking around the maternity car park trying to speed things up. It didn't speed things up and the ring was far too big. Three long and painful days later, the little darling was born and a few weeks later, I had the ring on my finger.

We finally got married four months, after Molly was born, at an intimate ceremony in a registry office on the fourth anniversary of the day we got together. The building in which we got married in has now been turned into a strip club, which is hilariously called 'Wiggle'. Yep, I got married in a strip club. Something my kids find highly amusing today, thankfully. Apart from the two friends we had as witnesses, we didn't tell anyone until after the 'ceremony', including my family. Most of our friends were doing a ski season abroad anyway, so a little text informing them of what we had done sparked a big celebration over there.

Unfortunately, my mum wasn't entirely ecstatic about not having an invite to my marriage ceremony, but we just didn't want a big fuss or a big audience and wanted the day to be about our commitment to each other, without spending copious amounts of money we didn't have to do just that. In fact, I think we spent about £200 in all, including the wedding rings and lunch. And just in case you were wondering, no, the rings weren't from a cracker or sweet packet and haven't disintegrated yet, and the lunch was at a proper restaurant with waiter and waitress service and everything! It was a really nice day and we very much enjoyed ourselves. Luckily, however, for my mum and dad, my sister had the full-on works for her wedding a couple of years later, so they were able to enjoy that day in every way possible.

We didn't have much money during this time and we were still quite young, so to keep ourselves sane, friends would often come around to ours to visit us so we didn't feel like we missed out on life in our twenties just because we had kids. Our parents were amazing at babysitting duties too, and Pete and I even managed to go to Glastonbury for the whole weekend and leave a six-week-old Dylan with my parents. Of course that was the first time he slept through the night too, my little angel.

Pete and I obviously didn't get as much sleep as Dylan that weekend as I am blaming the continued lack of sleep that weekend on the reason why it took us seven hours to find our car afterwards. Oh and why we had accidently left the inside car light on all weekend too, meaning we had a flat battery when we finally did find the car. I do try and look at the bright side of things and I'd like to say that walking around Glastonbury's entire perimeter twice and seeing the site from every angle possible was a beautiful thing to experience, but it certainly wasn't when extremely hung-over, tired, unusually unclean and arguing profusely.

Pete had a strong love of beer and whisky that caused some issues over the years, but we worked through it mostly.

I did have cause and courage to take the kids and leave him for a few weeks due to his continued behaviour whilst being fucking drunk, but he had a few sessions with a counsellor on the back of that and remarkably sorted his shit out. My marriage at that point was devastatingly over, but amazingly, he literally did a 180-degree life turn around and decided to occasionally only drink 'cooking beer', as he described it, from now in a bid to stop being such an arsehole and actually remember what he did and said during the evenings.

I think the realisation that he just might lose the kids and myself forever was strong enough for him to value us over booze and he kept to his word. His counsellor also told him to write a diary and upon reading that back to himself, he noticed that he was actually being a dick and I wasn't. That following year, I can honestly say was the best year we ever had together. For the first time, I genuinely felt like I could spend the rest of my life with this man. I know that sounds strange, seeing as though we were married with two kids by then and I did love him, but it wasn't until that point that I really, really believed I could be with this man for the rest of my days. Oh, the irony.

Now this brings me to a rather special day, what I now call 'Pete's day', which was just over a year after our mini separation. I know death isn't a particularly cheery subject and neither is it one that people like to talk about but I actually like talking about my death story so please laugh, cry, tut, sob, grin or just don't bother reading on, do whatever you want, it's apparently a free world. But I hope you do read on and you at least smile a little at my experience of life, death and a little bit more irony.

Chapter Three

A few weeks prior to Pete's day, the kids, Pete, Ruth and myself were all at my mother-in-law's discussing the film *Watership Down*, as I think it had been shown on television recently, and Pete came out with the sentence, "I want the song *Bright Eyes* to be played at my funeral, please."

To which my mother-in-law replied with a disapproving tut, "But that would make everyone cry!"

Pete's reply was, "Yes, I want everyone to cry at my funeral, I want everyone to be really bloody sad that I'm dead!" He had obviously been thinking about this, clearly displaying some issues.

Anyway, fast forward to Saturday, 9th February 2008. The sun was shining and it was a lovely day. Pete had worked a few hours in the morning whilst I had very kindly sorted out a pile of kid's toys and other such crap for him to take to the tip when he got home. After his tip trip he had lunch, a sandwich (ham and cheese) and crisps (steak flavoured McCoys), and then a mutual friend called Keith came around to call for Pete up as they had arranged to go for a motorbike ride that afternoon.

Keith had borrowed his brother-in-law's motorbike that day, and Pete had bought his motorbike six weeks previously as a reward to himself for working, so hard so they were both pretty excited to be going out on the bikes together. Pete had always wanted a motorbike and financially, we were finally able to afford one. Well, courtesy of the bank. He had also bought a lovely new tinted visor that was having its maiden voyage that day. I know he was extremely happy right then.

So, waving them off out the driveway that day with my final words to Pete, "have fun!" they rode off with what I can only imagine being rather large smiles on their faces. All that was left for me to do was get on with my day and do whatever parenting stuff needed doing. It was a beautiful sunny, boring, normal Saturday afternoon.

Now, if only I had remembered all those times that Pete had done something stupid like miss the nail and accidently hammer the same finger pretty much on a daily basis, drop a cement mixer on his foot whilst pulling it off a truck, brake the same finger on a cement mixer two weeks in a row to the confusion of the whole building site, step on a hedgehog bare foot in the garden, fall off his skateboard and loose a nipple, tombstone on his surfboard. If only I had remembered then I probably would have been that nagging wife and stepped in to plead, "Please don't get a motorbike darling, you're too clumsy and will more than likely have an accident on it. Possibly even die on it." I'm under no illusion that he probably wouldn't have listened to me but in hindsight, Pete 'the clumsy' should never ever have gotten a bloody motorbike.

Anyway, back to Pete's day and the slightly sad bit. Later on that normal Saturday afternoon whilst pottering around in the flat, I noticed a missed call a few minutes ago on my mobile phone from Keith, our friend that was out with Pete. *Slightly strange*, I thought, *why would he be calling me and not Pete?* So inquisitively, I instantly returned his call. It honestly didn't occur to me that anything could be wrong at that moment. Keith didn't answer, but a gentleman with a foreign accent did. Weird again.

I can't remember this guy's exact words to me on the phone, but it was something like, "I'm sorry, your husband has passed away."

It's really weird for me to think about this exact moment, because it was at this exact moment that my life took a different turn. It feels like a kind of kink or bend in the road or path of my life that changed everything. Right up until that precise second, my husband was alive and my life was normal. Same old shit, different day. That's how quick and easy things can change dramatically in life, in a spilt second.

Cliché, I know, but so true. In that split second, it felt like my life got smashed into a billion pieces.

"I'm sorry, who did you want to speak to?" came my automatic disbelieving response, adrenaline and all kinds of chemical reactions starting to make their presence known within my body.

"You need to speak to your friend," said the guy, obviously not wanting to repeat the information he had just informed me of. Understandable.

Seriously, what the fuck was going on! Why was this person telling me this shit? My brain couldn't and didn't want to compute this. Understandable again. The phone was passed to Keith and as soon as I heard his voice, I knew. That's when I got that 'sinking' feeling and a kind of 'click' into reality. I think that's why all these memories are still so strong and vivid ten years later. Keith told me to get someone with me as soon as I could. I found out afterwards that the guy I first spoke to was a doctor who was one of the first on the scene as he was in a car travelling just behind the accident and got caught up in the queue of traffic, poor guy. I also now know that when I spoke to Keith on the phone, he was holding Pete's hand, giving me that little connection. The time was 3.52 pm on Saturday, 9th February 2008, and Pete had been dead for a couple of minutes.

Chapter Four

The accident was totally Pete's fault. Witnesses said he hadn't been speeding and was riding sensibly prior to the accident. For some reason, going round a slight left-hand bend, he had wandered across onto the other side of the road just as a People carrier came round the corner and hit him face on, well chest on, to be accurate. Where it happened there is a right hand turn just up from the accident site, so the road kind of looked like it bent round to the right and not left, but Pete knew the road and Keith was in front, which meant Pete would have seen him if he went right, so God knows why he did it. Only he will know why he just didn't follow the road and stay on his side, but all we do know is that his last word was probably, "FUCK!" In actual fact, he probably only got as far as making the sound, "FU…"

So straight after that informative phone call, I went on autopilot. I remember feeling instantly very, very alone, so I shakily marched right into the lounge where the kids were happily watching some annoying children's TV programme and simply blurted it out. I wasn't sure of the protocol for telling an eight-year-old and a six-year-old child that their daddy had just died, as it's not in any parenting book I'd read; so I just kind of came out with that fact. Of course, they couldn't comprehend what I had just told them. I couldn't comprehend what I was telling them either, but I think the look on my face made them realise crying was the correct thing to do. Molly says she only starting crying because her big brother did. A three-way confused, emotional hug followed for a few minutes.

Then I took Keith's advice and the next thing I did was call my sister-in-law, Pete's sister, Ruth. I didn't blurt it out to her straight away on the phone, oh no, not like I did with my two young kids. I simply asked her what she was up to, to which she replied, "Just on my way back from Harrison's (her godson) birthday party, shall I come round?"

"Yes," I replied. She didn't ask me how I was, what I was up to or anything. She says she just knew something was wrong and didn't need to ask on the phone. She arrived in about five minutes, thankfully, where more confused hugs and tears followed. Then to phone Pete's mum, Jenny, and invite her around for some bad news.

The hours that followed are a blur, but basically a lot of bemused crying, hugging, cigarette smoking, vodka drinking and swearing was done by Ruth, Jenny and myself. We seemed to have instantly developed Tourette's because swear words kept spontaneously blurting out of our mouths at quite a high volume as the news started to sink in. Again, there is no protocol for such an event, so all I can describe that evening as, is being weird. I felt different, everything looked different and I just couldn't settle or concentrate on anything. I felt like I should be doing something, but had no idea what that something was.

Time felt weird too. Time didn't matter at all where I had been used to time really mattering. Always having things to do, places to be and never having enough time to do it all in, especially with a husband and two kids. But now, that evening time was totally irrelevant. To my parents, time was very relevant that evening. They had moved to Spain a few years previously, bit of an extreme way of getting out babysitting, I know, but they had to wait until the following day to get a flight back to see us and spend precious 'time' with us.

The following morning, after an obvious, tearful pillow hugging, Tourette's-ticking, sleepless night, we decided to tell the rest of the family and all our friends. After some vodka and fags for breakfast as courage, my sister-in-law being the strong one, started making the calls. It became evident pretty quickly that one of two responses would come back from each and every person after informing them of Pete's death. The first response being, "You're joking!" Oh no, sick joke if we were, but sadly, we're not joking, he really did die yesterday and the second response being, "say that again?" and of course, repeating that fact is so much more enjoyable than saying it just the once.

We liked to think of that next day like a ripple effect. When you told those first few people, they would tell more people then they would tell more people and so on. Telling that first person was the initial drop in the water and the rippling effect is everyone finding out after that. That ripple effect can go on sometime, especially when it's a young, well-liked person who knew a lot of people. But at least we didn't have to tell everyone ourselves. Good friends helped with the ripple. We almost had to write a list of people to tell and tick them off when the deed had been, done because phoning to tell them twice wouldn't had been ideal for both parties either. Most conversations with friends after that started with the words, "have you heard?"

Being the close group of friends that we were, Ruth and I knew everyone would want to be together that day, so a gathering at our local pub, "The Malt and Hops" was arranged for that Sunday evening. I can honestly say I've never seen my friends looking so shit. I remember looking in the mirror prior to going out and thinking, "Jesus you actually look like your husband has just died", so I doubt I looked much better. Anyway, this was the first time leaving my flat since the news and the first time of seeing people outside that bubble. The first of many firsts we'd have to go through.

Chapter Five

The time before the funeral was a very weird time, a time that feels like you're in limbo. There's so much to do yet so much you don't want to do. Preparation for the celebration of a life yet the organisation for the cancellation of a life. During this time, I almost felt like I was in an untouchable bubble and things just seemed to go my way. Things like traffic lights stayed on green until I'd driven through them and people I met who didn't know me were just generally really nice, not something that happens regularly. I honestly felt like I was wearing a badge. Or maybe it was just the state of my face; looking in the mirror was really not a pleasant thing. Or maybe I just didn't care about those things anymore. My priorities had instantly changed the moment Pete died too. Anyway, it was a bit unnerving how life just seemed to run so smoothly and well during this time. It was a massively shit thing to happen and I really felt like I deserved everyone and everything being nice to me. If ever there was a time to milk these niceties, it certainly was now.

The funeral home asked us if we wanted to see Pete before the funeral and it was agreed that we did. I knew it was going to be hard seeing him lying dead in a coffin and that image will be stuck in my memory forever but honestly, I have plenty of other harrowing memories in their now anyway. One being the sight of my mother-in-law's face; her face after learning her only son was dead will be etched in my memory forevermore. So, actually her normal day-to-day face isn't too bad to look at now.

Pete was going to be cremated, so it really was the last time to see his physical self as well before he became a box of ash. I kind of needed to make sure that he was definitely dead too and it wasn't just a big prank being played on us all, so again after some vodka and fags as courage and swear words as a pep talk, Ruth, Jenny and myself paid him a visit in the funeral home.

We were taken into a little room where he had been prepared for viewing. My first thought was, "what the hell have they done to his hair!" Now he was very particular and extremely conscientious about his hair and oh my, I guess they had tried their best, but they had clearly got it ever so wrong. Of course, they'd never met him alive, so it was all guesswork for them; they had given him a big bouffant hairdo. And he seemed to be dressed in the lining of the coffin, which was pale blue in colour with ruffles and lace around the cuffs and chest area. I think it was made to look like a suit, but they'd actually made him look like a 1970s playboy.

Before I went in to see Pete, I had all these grand ideas about holding his hand, stroking his hair, kissing his forehead and maybe talking to him, but in reality, none of this happened. I managed to lightly touch is hand, which was the coldest thing I have ever touched, and it properly scared me. I tried to kiss his forehead, but only got as far as kissing his hair, chickened out and made a hasty retreat. We'd all had enough after about two minutes and were back to drinking vodka and smoking fags within about 10 minutes. It was a massive shock seeing him and it felt like another kick in the life again, but I think I needed that little jolt back into reality to help with the realignment, so I could try and begin my recovery.

I made an executive decision and decided not to give the kids the option of seeing Pete's dead body. I didn't even tell them we went to see him until years later and again I felt and still do feel that I made the correct call on that one. Kids ask lots of questions, so imagine the questions we would have had to deal with. "Why is Daddy lying in a box? Why does Daddy feel like ice? Why is Daddy's hair like that? Why is Daddy dressed like a clown? Can we take Daddy home?" And because the kids were so young, there was that danger that their first-ever memory would be exactly that, Daddy sleeping in a box dressed like a pimp.

People were so beautifully nice around this time too and we received so many cards and flowers, we could have opened up a florist's. Because of the timing of Pete's death, Valentine's Day was the most ironic one yet. Receiving flowers from men other than my husband, dinner and chocolates being delivered to us by my next-door neighbour and spending the whole day and evening with my mother-in-law and sister-in-law.

For the funeral, we decided we all needed new outfits as we hoped this might make us feel slightly better about the occasion. We thought Dylan might need some male company for his shopping trip, as the poor boy had mostly been in the presence of three highly emotional females and his little sister for a while now. And we probably would have been really embarrassing and all cried when we saw him try on his little funeral suit. So our next-door neighbour very kindly took him on a less embarrassing lads' suit-shopping trip.

So, female shopping trip for funeral clobber for the rest of us, although we did drag Dylan along with us too. I had bought a new dress and coat, and we were all now in the shoe shop with me trying on some boots to complete my outfit when the poor young girl that was serving us asked with a smile, "Is it for a special occasion?" A pause from us all followed as we tried very quickly to decide how to reply and who would reply to this question. So, informing her that it was for the funeral of my husband, Ruth's brother, Jenny's son and these young kid's father, she did the obligatory subconscious head tilt whilst saying, "Oh, I'm so sorry", that I had learnt everyone does when you tell them really sad news. A slightly subdued and awkwardly polite boot fitting followed.

Preparations for the funeral included a run through by the priest in the church. My mother-in-law is a very religious lady and had been a member of the congregation at this church for many years, and Father Dunne had been the priest at the church for many years too. He was a super sweet, mad old

Irish guy, had baptised Dylan and Molly, so knew the family very well. Therefore, the run through was going as well as can be expected and the lovely Father Dunne was taking Jenny, Ruth and myself through the service, so we would know when and how things would happen on the day.

We had easily chosen the music we wanted playing, and of course, that included the track Pete had wanted everyone to cry to. In order to get the volume correct on the day, we had brought along the track we wanted playing at the beginning of the service. This was, of course, the music that we would be leading the coffin in to. The song was Pete's favourite at the time and sounded amazing, resonating around the empty church. I really got lost in my thoughts of Pete, as it was his favourite tune at that time and struggled to hold back the tears. Luckily enough, Father Dunn brought us swiftly back into reality when he began expressing his appreciation for the tune by Dad dancing quite weirdly to it right in front of us, exclaiming that it was 'really rather good'. The track is Groove Armada's cover of *Crazy For You*, originally by Madonna.

So, trying not to giggle, as that would be inappropriate at this point, Father Dunne then took us into the back room of the church, as he wanted to show us what he would be wearing on the day. As he opened the cupboard door, imagine our surprise again when he let out a little noisy fart, without any acknowledgement at all. Now, you may think, *priests don't fart, it was probably the cupboard door making the noise*, but let me assure you, it was a definite fart. Father Dunne was probably thinking he got away with it as he opened the cupboard door at the same time, but we know a fart when we hear one. Confirmation also came with the 'don't you two dare!' look from my mother-in-law.

Therefore, this situation being pretty surreal already, I can only describe the following half hour or so as complete torture. I was totally unable to look at Ruth, and she was unable to look at me. All I could see was Ruth's shoulders shaking up and down, and I knew we would not be able to make eye contact for a good while.

Now, feeling highly inappropriate with the image of a farting Father Dunn dancing at the front of the church and really trying the hardest I ever have not to explode into fits of giggles, we were taken through to Father Dunn's house to sit down quietly and make the final preparations for the order of service. Yay, just what we all needed: A small quiet room to be in with our thoughts. I still couldn't look at Ruth or my mother-in-law for the entirety of the meeting that followed, as there was that background danger we would burst out into laughter as soon as we locked eyes whilst chatting about the order of service for Pete's bloomin' funeral! The only silver lining was the pain we were in from trying to stifle laughter was easily disguised as the pain of grief. Bonus!

Thankfully, surreal funeral run through was done and the music and hymns chosen; now to choose a photo for the front of the order of service. To be honest, this was a relatively easy decision, because every photo ever taken of Pete, he had his eyes either half open or totally closed, or the photo was of him intoxicated, so he was either cross-eyed or his eyes were pointing in totally different directions. So when we found the only photo of him where you could see his gorgeous blue eyes, and they were both looking directly at the camera, we knew that was the one and breathed a sigh of relief that we had actually found a suitable one.

Our wedding 27th February 2002

The boys before the paddle out at Pete's wake

The paddle out

Dylan looking at the paddle out

Pete's plaque on the memorial bench on Boscombe Pier

Pete at Bestival 2007

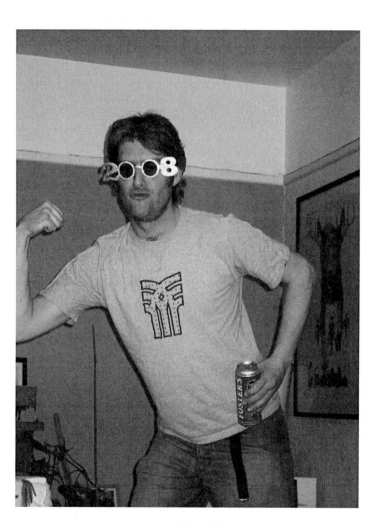

Pete NYE 2008

Pete, Dylan and Molly on Christmas Eve 2006

Nicola and Pete

Sarah Boardman (my top trumps friend) and Rob Matthews
(17/6/78 – 19/3/12)

Chapter Six

I actually quite enjoyed the funeral. Besides the obvious fact that it was nice to get it over with, we all had our hair done that morning and were all wearing our new outfits and miraculously looked pretty good for the first time since death day. It really is amazing what make-up can achieve! The day felt bizarre and a bit dreamlike, but I felt quite good and strangely confident. We had been preparing for that day for the last two and a half weeks, so I think most of my feelings were relief to have finally got there. And of course, I couldn't wait to see what moves Father Dunne might bust out for the real deal.

The funeral was an early morning service and on the way to church, we passed a friend who had stopped at the shops before the funeral. Upon seeing him, we knocked on the car window, waved with smiles on our faces and then realised where we were when he awkwardly smiled and waved back; we were in the funeral procession. So with everyone in the church, we got ready for the grand entrance for the man of the moment. Six good friends were the pallbearers and had the job of wheeling Pete into the church. Just before they did, they spun the coffin around, so he could do one last 360 on a set of wheels.

The church was absolutely packed and besides the sniffs and rustling of tissues, you could have literally heard a pin drop. There were some beautiful readings and lovely things said about Pete. The friend that read the eulogy wore a suit and flip flops and the kids had wanted to get up and say something too, so like arseholes, we let them. We knew what they were going to say as we printed it all out on card and everything, but it was tough to hear those words for the first time from two small children that had just lost their daddy. The funeral of a 31-year-old not being sad enough, here is what the kids got up to say:

"Dad, you were the greatest dad ever
And we will miss you so much.
You died doing something you loved
And we were all so proud of you.
We'll keep you alive in all our happy memories
And especially in our hearts.
Thank you, Dad."

Dylan, eight years old

"Dad, we really loved you
And all that you did for us.
Dad, we really love you still
Now that you are in Heaven.
We will see you again when we are in Heaven
And, until then, we will miss you lots."

Molly, six years old.

Funeral completed and onto the wake. The local pub, The Grange, was the venue, and I can safely say we all had a bloody good time. We had music, dancing, fireworks and plenty of alcohol. We even had a trip down onto the beach where a lot of the boys took to their surfboards and went in the sea to release some flowers for him. One friend even went in without a wetsuit on and due to it being the end of February, he was a little pink and shivery when he came, out but that shows how much love there was for this man. It was a really good send off and I know he would have been looking down, or up, and be very proud of everyone's efforts that day.

A couple of months after the funeral, Ruth, the kids and myself were driving back home from somewhere and noticed some fireworks going off. Due to it not being anywhere near bonfire night, I made a remark wondering why fireworks would be going off then. One of the kids said, "I wonder if they're for a funeral?"

I replied, a little bit shocked, "Seriously, who has fireworks at a funeral!" Errr, we did, for Dad's funeral, the kids reminded me! Oh shit, so we did! Short-term memory loss is a factor to remember when grieving.

I mentioned we had music at the wake. Well, it was more like a wake party with a sound system, a DJ and a high volume of music. The funeral was on a Wednesday and The Grange was also a small hotel, so there were some people staying in the rooms above the bar. The wake party went on fairly late I guess, and we probably weren't being particularly quiet at this point, but the hotel residents had the audacity to complain about the noise. We put them in their place and told them that it was a wake and we were trying to grieve, how rude!

Sometime after the funeral, probably around that springtime, a group of friends, the kids and myself were in The Grange, quietly enjoying a pint or two. Dylan was outside in the beer garden with Keith and a few other mates, kicking a football about quite happily, as he loves football, and I was sat in the bar with Molly, chatting with more friends. The next thing I know, a lady I've never met before approached me with tears rolling down her face and told me how sorry she was to hear about my husband. Slightly confused, I comforted this poor crying stranger, told her everything was okay and handed her some tissues.

It transpired that she had made a comment to Dylan outside about how lovely it was to see a father and son playing so nicely together, to which Dylan had innocently corrected her and stated that Keith wasn't his dad, his dad was dead, before carrying on with his football game. Dylan had been totally unfazed by this. However, this poor lady had been quite upset by this.

It was at The Grange pub that we began the scattering of Pete's ashes. Well, it was kind of accidental, really. When we picked up the box of ashes from the funeral directors, we of course decided to take him straight to the pub. Pete had spent a fair few hours of his life there, so it seemed fitting to take his ashes for one last visit to his local. The kids, Ruth, Jenny and myself stood there quietly having a drink outside, staring at this box, wondering what was actually inside it and what Pete now looked like. Curiosity eventually won, so we held our breaths and carefully opened the box. Sure enough, it was filled with grey, fine ash. Don't know what we were actually expecting, but it didn't disappoint. Upon closing the box, a little bit of Pete fell on the floor, thus beginning (accidentally) the scattering of his ashes.

Due to Pete being a surfer and general lover of the ocean, we decided the best place to scatter the rest of his ashes was at sea. Personally, I didn't want a grave to visit or feel guilty if I didn't visit, so with Pete at sea, wherever we are in the world, we can look out and remember him. Also, friends around the world would also be able to do the same, so a big ashes-scattering boat party was arranged for that June. He was kept in a box in the lounge on the sideboard for four months until then.

In keeping with the funeral celebrations, we had a DJ, dance floor, booze and loads of friends and family attending. There happened to be a few poles dotted around the dance floor on this boat, obviously for structural purposes, so a six-year-old Molly entertained us by innocently swinging around those. We got the boat to take us out to Old Harry Rocks where we all gathered on the top deck for the ceremonial transition and final, final goodbye. The song we chose to play for this departure was *Starlight* by Muse. We wanted Keith to do the honours and tip Pete into the sea.

First into the sea, though, were some roses thrown in by the family. The idea that we would watch these float away into the distance, bobbing over the gentle waves of the ocean, was soon quashed as they sunk immediately. Being ever so slightly disappointed by this, we quickly decided to move onto the ashes. All was pretty calm, so with a few lovely words and deep breaths, Keith began tipping the box to release Pete into his final resting place, his favourite place to be, in the sea. Yes, you guessed it, just as a massive gust of wind came and swept Pete all around and onto us. Keith was wearing a black jacket prior to the tipping, which suddenly turned grey. Molly loudly exclaimed she had some of Daddy in her eye, most people got a bit of Pete in their drinks, my mum got some in her coat pocket, which she found on her return to Spain, but mostly, Pete went straight into everyone's mouths. Not sure how much actually made it into the sea, but I'm pretty sure we all ingested a little bit of Pete that day.

Chapter Seven

For the past 11-Pete-free years, my kids have been my inspiration and motive for life. They will probably disagree with that statement, and they like to tell people that they have dragged themselves up, and on a weekly basis they threaten to buy me a one-way ticket to Switzerland, but I do strongly believe if it weren't for those pesky kids, I would have sunk into a pit of depression and not achieved half the things I have done. I really can't thank them enough for being accidentally put into my life when they were.

One of the things the kids asked me quite early on after Pete died was whether I was going to get a single bed now. Their reason for asking me as they told me was because I was never going to get married again, so had no need for a double bed anymore. Although, they did inform me I could marry a celebrity now! Not sure if they had a particular one in mind though. They really did help me through, spotting when I was trying to have a private cry in my bedroom and saying with a tut to their other sibling, "Mum's crying again, she needs a hug", before both of them giving me a big bear hug.

At the time of Pete's death, both kids were attending a Roman Catholic primary school. Now, I'm not religious in the slightest. I'm not against religion, I think whatever makes you happy then worship it, believe in it, idolise it or whatever, but I don't think you have to go sit in a certain building and chant certain words from a certain book to make you a good person. But the church community that was linked to the school was totally brilliant at this time and I cannot thank them enough for the love and support we all received.

The kids wanted to go straight back to school after Pete died. Getting back to normality as soon as possible after such a traumatic event is what I wanted to do too, so we were all back to our normal working and school lives within two weeks of his death. Back to doing the school run, feeling like a celebrity with all those eyes on us and seeing the gentle nudges within parent groups, whispering, "That's the one", in between lots of lovely well wishes from tearful strangers.

The entire school went to weekly mass on Thursday afternoons and certain parents of certain classes were invited to attend and sit with their children during certain masses during the school year. Jenny, Ruth and I were invited to a special school mass for Pete where we were given some lovely poems and letters that some of the other kids in school had done for Dylan and Molly. It really was heartwarming and highly emotional. We were the only parents in that mass surrounded by the whole of the primary school kids, so we stuck out a bit, especially as we were sat right in the middle of the church. At the beginning of the mass, just after everyone was seated, we heard a little voice moan from the row directly behind us, "Oh great, now I can't see!" We did turn and smile as this little child blushed and sank down quite far into the pew, obviously realising he had said that slightly louder than he'd intended.

As heart breaking as it is, seeing two small children lose their dad, their innocence always shines through and makes you giggle. Some friends in Australia very kindly sent over a photo album with some stickers in for the kids. Molly was sat working on her creation one day when she turned and asked, "How do you spell 'dead'?" She was making a caption out of the stickers under a photo that read, 'DAD IS DEAD', but had got stuck on the word 'dead'.

When a child so young loses someone so close, it is totally normal for his or her grief journey to not start until about two years after this event. This was certainly true in Molly's case. One night at a tearful bedtime, she told me she didn't have any memories of her own of her daddy. All the things she could remember about him had come from people telling her their memories of him. I went through as many memories as I could with her that night, but none of them were hers. As much as I could try to help, I distressingly knew I really couldn't help her at all on this one.

Until one day, she unconsciously came out with a little story of her own about her daddy, to which I quickly informed her with a massive relief that there it was, she did have a memory of her own of him. That one memory of hers that she has had from then on is of her daddy drawing a smiley face on his naked butt in a blue felt tip pen and moonying her several times across her open bedroom door before he got into the bath. The one thing I remember about this is that it was a Friday evening and he had been to the pub for some after-work beers, so was a little pissed when doing so and after said bath, I found a blue imprint of said smiley face on the bottom of our nice white bath.

Chapter Eight

Milestones and firsts are unwanted events that loom up and smack you in the face, and the emotional rollercoaster that is grief really is unbelievable. Obviously, there is sadness and lots of crying to start with, which kind of never really goes away; it just gets less and less severe and less regular as time goes on. Also to begin with, there is a lot of anger and bemusement as to why this has happened. I got annoyed with Pete for leaving me to bring up two children all on my own.

I now was the one that had to always do bath time, dinnertime, bedtime stories, the lot. I even had to do things, like always be the one to take the bins out, do all the food shopping, all the cooking and cleaning, even clean the car and sort out the Ministry of Transport (MOT), etc. I also now had 100% of the responsibility of the kids too, had to do ALL of the decisionmaking and go to all of the parent's evenings and school productions, alone and emotional. Cheers Pete, I didn't sign up for that when I birthed them!

Then mixed in with this anger and disbelief is always sadness. Sadness that Pete missed Molly losing her first baby tooth, sadness that Pete never saw Dylan get his first chest hair. Sadness that he never saw either of them get to double figures, leave primary school for secondary school, leave secondary school for sixth form, leave sixth form for university. Sadness that the first thing the kids think of when they see fireworks is, "I wonder if it's for a funeral?" Sadness that my 'how long ago' gauge has now been set to whether it happened prior to or after Pete's death!

Then mixed with all the anger, sadness and disbelief comes a relief and slight happiness that I can now watch whatever I want on television and I don't have to kick anyone in bed for keeping me awake, snoring. An extreme relief for myself and Molly, because Pete always said that when Molly started dating, he would get a tattoo on his forehead, so he would be that intimidating father, meaning no one would mess with his daughter. Slightly happy I have one less person's clothes to wash and the food-shopping bill would be a lot less. Upon hearing friends moan about their partners and getting a little smug 'thank fuck' feeling inside. Then of course feeling guilty about feeling that way.

Then another emotion arrives, feeling scared and afraid of course about the future but also when, for the first time since Pete dying, we have an eight-legged creature in the flat that has to be removed around screaming kids. And when a light bulb goes and trips the circuit plunging us into total darkness (yes, of course, this had to happen when it's pitch black outside and a couple of months after Pete's day), causing the kids to become hysterical and start crying and screaming because they think I am totally incapable of changing a light bulb and illuminating the flat ever again.

The emotional roller coaster goes on and on and on, and the first year is all about firsts. Having your first birthday without them, having their first birthday without them actually aging, the first Christmas and New Year without them. My first first was my wedding anniversary, my tenth wedding anniversary, which was two and a half weeks after Pete's day. Luckily, the traditional gifts for 10 years of marriage is only tin or aluminium, so I'd have been a bit more pissed off if that was emerald or gold but needless to say, February is my least favourite month of the year now. Pete's death day, Valentine's Day and my wedding anniversary all in one month. Silver lining, at least it's over quicker than the other months in the year!

Back on to that emotional roller coaster. When Pete first died, a few people told me that it takes about two years to get over loosing someone you love. Because of this, I was kind of excited and relieved to finally be getting to that second anniversary and was actually looking forward to it. Those two years had been a long time coming, so when it got to that day, imagine my surprise, sadness, annoyance, disbelief and guilt when I didn't feel miraculously better. It actually made me feel worse therefore making that second anniversary my least favourite of all the anniversaries I've ever had to endure over the years.

Another thing that gave me those mixed, guilty, annoying feelings was the lovely messages people had written in the book we passed around at Pete's wake. Everyone had written some super sweet things, but maybe a little too sweet and nice. I mean, just because he died didn't mean he was an amazing human being all the time he was alive, he was a grumpy, sarcastic twat a lot of the time. He'd been put on this pedestal just because he was dead which annoyed me, in turn making me annoyed at myself. It wasn't his fault he was dead. Well, actually, it was, but I'm sure he would have chosen life instead of death if he'd been given the option that day. The endless circle of emotions is very confusing and definitely shit.

Chapter Nine

People have asked me over the years if I've ever felt Pete's presence around me. To be honest, the answer is no. I'd like to think he is somehow looking after us, especially the kids, but it kind of weirds me out to think that he's around me, watching me. I have heard noises in the flat over the years that sound like someone walking down the hallway or getting up off the sofa, and Dylan did hear the front door shut once when he was alone in the flat about 10 minutes before I walked in the front door, but to keep us all from being highly terrorstricken, I've put it down to the normal creepy noises buildings make when you're alone in them.

One evening a few months after Pete's death day having put the kids to bed, Molly came back into the lounge and asked if anyone just looked round her bedroom door and checked on her? Nobody had. Dylan was in his bedroom and I had been in the lounge with Ruth. No one else was in the flat. She said she saw someone with blue eyes peering around her door, thought it was me telling her to go to sleep, so she turned away quickly and waited for me to speak. When I didn't speak, she looked back and no one was there. I'm pretty sure it was Pete checking on her, which does give us some comfort and makes me feel strangely peaceful. Either that, or worryingly we do actually have a copycat ghost in the flat.

I have, however, had a couple of dreams over the years with Pete in. One dream was nice and it consisted of Pete and I holding hands and kissing whilst spinning around gazing into each other's eyes. I know it sounds corny, but that is the actual dream I had and I really, really felt like I was with him in this dream. It was so nice to feel him and be with him again whilst I was asleep, but horrific when I woke up and realised it was just a dream and I would never feel that again. It was like finding out he was dead, all over again.

The other Pete dream I had was just as much of a head fuck, but in a totally different way. Pete was an electrician by trade when he died, so left me with a few tools that I probably couldn't name let alone know how to use. A friend who was working with Pete at the time was amazing and organised an auction to sell Pete's tools to people he had worked with over the years, thus making us some well-needed money.

I can't remember how this particular dream started, but it seemed so real again. My current situation in real life at the time and in my dream was exactly the same until all of a sudden, Pete jumped out from behind the sofa with a big grin on his face and shouted, "Surprise!!! I'm not really dead; I've been alive all along and was just hiding." My immediate thought in my dream wasn't *thank the lord, I'm so relieved you're alive!* It was *but you can't be, all these people have been so nice to me and sold your tools. They have given me money, which I've spent so what am I going to do now? I can't give it back to them!* Panic setting in.

So my feelings whilst asleep in this dream was not happiness that Pete was actually alive, but panic about having to find and give this money back to everyone. With that thought, I thankfully awoke with the realisation and relief that Pete hadn't been hiding, he was actually still dead and I didn't have to find the money to give back. *Phew*, I thought. And then my next thought was obvious guilt that for a split second I had actually been relieved that Pete was dead.

Chapter Ten

When someone departs this world, they leave a lot of life admin for their loved ones left behind to delete and cancel. Luckily, Pete hadn't left me with any secret subscriptions to stumble upon and quickly unsubscribe, as I can see that being a fairly awkward situation to have to deal with at an already problematic time. So, upon phoning all the bulk standard companies you need to inform them a person no longer exists, you then have to confirm this statement by sending them either the original death certificate or a certified copy of the death certificate to confirm their death. It's a fairly long-winded and laborious process, which has to be repeated many times over.

We received Pete's final certificate of achievement, his death certificate, through the post from Wiltshire County Council's registry office not long after his death, and seeing it in black-and-white again felt like a small smack in the face, back to reality. The compliment slip that was included in the envelope with the death certificate from Wiltshire County Council was a little ironic and did make me chuckle. Their tag line was 'improving life in Wiltshire'. I could almost hear Pete's voice saying, "Typical, lying council bastards, my life didn't see an improvement in Wiltshire that day!"

Pete had only purchased the bike and relative bike insurance about six weeks prior to death day and of course, this was one of the first companies I contacted to inform them of his death to ensure the cover was cancelled. Mistakenly thinking this had been dealt with and forgetting about it, nearly a year later, bizarrely, dead Pete received a letter from this bike insurance company with his insurance renewal details on. Yet again I phoned them to inform of Pete and the bike's termination so insurance definitely not needed; an apology came with the explanation of failure to pass the information on to the renewals team at the time of my first phone call. They only had one simple fucking job to do!

Junk mail is another pain in the ass. Just when you think it's all been taken care of, another shitty, brightly coloured bit of cheap, smelly paper arrives on the doormat addressed to your deceased loved one. Honestly, I think it was years before that stopped. I did think about getting a rather morbid stamp made up which said, 'RETURN TO SENDER—DECEASED' to save any hand ache from writing it so much. We had quite a few cold calls early on asking to speak to Mr Happé. My favourite by far is the "our records show you or someone in your household has had an accident in the past three years, that wasn't your fault" call. We've all had them and of course, we've all had some fun over the years with our responses to those particular calls, but even my sardonic conversations with the expectant cold caller has got a bit monotonous now. The most persistent thing, however, has been emails. Pete and I shared an email address and no matter how many times I press the unsubscribe link, eleven years on I still get the odd email that begins, 'Dear Peter'. I am hopeful that the General Data Protection Regulation (GDPR) bollocks will sort that out once and for all.

Weird and not so wonderful coincidences have a tendency to happen too at really relevant times. About four months after death day, I had a message left on my telephone answerphone from a lady informing me of some details about a funeral of someone I'd never heard of. She obviously had the wrong number and presumed she was leaving a message on a funeral director's answerphone. This had never happened before and has never happened since.

Also, not really been witness to any road traffic accidents over my previous 31 years of life; some poor little old lady got a little knock from a car right outside our flat about two weeks before the first anniversary of Pete's death day. Unfortunately, she was lying in the road for quite some time while being attended to and thankfully, I don't think it was too serious, but it obviously brought back some unwanted images and poignant feelings at an already exceptional, emotional time.

Unfortunately, within that first year, Ruth also had a minor motorbike accident happen right in front of her car when she had a nine-year-old Dylan in the front passenger seat. No one was hurt, thankfully, although a little road rage followed from the young guy who's bike had been hit. Ruth had to quickly but politely go over and ask this guy to 'calm the fudge down' as the little boy, avidly watching the situation unfold in the front of her car, had recently lost his dad in a far worse motorbike accident than the one that had just occurred. Perspective gained and handbags swiftly put away.

Because Pete's accident was a Road Traffic Accident (RTA), there had to be an inquest into his death to establish the exact cause. These never happen quickly either, so around two years after death day, the inquest was finally heard. To be honest, we didn't find anything out that we hadn't already known and a verdict of accidental death was confirmed. One of the first witnesses on the scene was asked some questions at the inquest and had described the male who had been hit, upon taking his helmet off, as being in his forties, which did make Ruth and I chuckle a little. Poor Pete, he was pretty much a total silver fox by then, but he was only 31-years-old. Tough paper round, perhaps!

Also, present at the inquest was the lady who had been driving the car that had hit and ultimately killed Pete. A difficult day for all of us to face, but all we felt like we could do as soon as we saw this poor lady was give her a hug and tell her that we didn't blame her at all for Pete's death. The formality of the inquest didn't last long appreciatively, so after saying our goodbyes to this lady (pretty sure she never wanted to see us again), her husband and the family liaison police officer, who had been through the whole thing with us too, we decided to go to a local café or restaurant for some well-earned lunch and try and draw a line under all the formalities that had now been completed. Fingers crossed!

The establishment we chose for lunch was quite busy, but we managed to spot one free table, so we quickly went and sat down at it. Can you guess who was sitting on the very next table? Of course she was, the lady, who was driving that fateful car and her husband. We had already committed to sitting at that table by the time we realised they were there and it would have been pretty rude and a very obvious retreat if we had backed out of the restaurant just because we saw them there. A slightly awkward beginning to lunch followed. As it turned out, during that lunch, we had a lovely chat with them and got to know them a bit, which I think helped on both sides. We haven't had any contact with that lady since that day, but I do wish her all the best and I do think about her and send her a little love on every anniversary of Pete's day.

Chapter Eleven

There's not just life admin to sort out when someone dies, but there is just a shit load of life-everything to sort out. Clothes are a highly emotional memory of the recently deceased and Pete had left behind quite a lot of t-shirts for me to cry over. So, to try and reduce the amount I may have used as future tissues, I got close friends to come around and take a t-shirt each as a small souvenir of him. It certainly dented the pile, but due to the sheer volume he had accumulated over the years, I was still left with a fair few, which are still to this day gathering dust under my bed.

I mistakenly decided to keep a few other items of Pete's clothing that I thought Dylan might want to wear when he grew big enough. When he got big enough to wear them, I cheerfully gave them to him, but all he did when he saw them was laugh a lot at the mere suggestion of even trying them on. Luckily, however, not all was lost; Molly needed some new pyjamas, so I palmed a few t-shirts and old jumpers off onto her instead, which she still wears today.

It's a really difficult decision to know when to sort out a person's belongings after they've passed, as again it's not something you have any motivation to do or were expecting to do at any time in your life. What do you keep and do you throw any of it away? We all keep junk or childhood memorabilia that means something to us, but not a thing to anyone else. What to give to charity and would it be weird to think about a stranger wearing his clothes and shoes? What if I would see an item of his clothing being worn by a stranger down the street? Okay, the odds are stacked against that happening, but all his belongings would just be collecting more dust and taking up valuable room in boxes under my bed. We didn't live in a massive flat, so space should really be limited to the living.

One large dilemma I gave myself was when I was going to take off my wedding and engagement rings. One minute I'd lovingly think, *I'm going to keep them on forever*, and then I'd get upset and angry and think, *I'm taking them off right now as I'm no longer married, my husband's dead and I am a widow, so it's pointless wearing them*. And then I'd get all sentimental and want to wear them on a necklace or get the (small) diamond made into something I could wear on a necklace, but I'd also want to give them to Molly one day in the future. In the end, I settled for taking them off straight after the funeral and putting them back in the ring box Pete had presented them to me in. I didn't feel married anymore, I felt alone and single so I felt that this was the right thing for me to do, a mini closure for me at that time. I also felt that if I was still wearing them, people would presume I was married and presumably ask me about my husband during an innocent conversation. Although, by then, I quite liked weirding people out by telling them I was widowed when they asked, it wasn't a conversation I would have chosen to have anymore than I had to.

I still do quite like weirding people out about my current marital status, 'widowed', as it's not a common one for someone of my age and it certainly is a conversation starter. When I tell people now, I still get that obligatory head tilt with the standard, "I'm sorry to hear that", but I quickly follow it up with, "It's okay, it was eleven years ago now", just so they don't think I'm going to burst into floods of tears and that it is actually okay to ask me about it. We all have a morbid curiosity, me included, and we want to know how someone has died, so what I have learnt over the years is to reel off a list of statements, so they don't have to ask or let their imaginations run wild. They generally consist of, "it was a motorbike accident", "the accident was Pete's fault", "the kids were six and eight years old at the time", "he was 31 years old", "we're all doing really well now", "the kids are amazing and doing great, they are 17 and 19 years old now" and "no, I haven't met anyone else yet and I'm actually really happy now."

A few questions I have asked myself over the years include can you only fall in love once? There may well be plenty more fish in the sea, but would I ever have or be allowed to have what I had with Pete again in my life? Would it just be greedy if I did? Would I feel guilty if I did? How much time is acceptable to leave between death of a partner and the start of a new relationship? If I were to ever get married again, would I change my surname...again? Is Pete looking down and only sending weird and not-quite-right-in-the-head single men my way for his own amusement? More importantly, would I ever be able to get drunk ever again without becoming an emotional sobbing wreck?

Chapter Twelve

After Pete died, I found out a lot of people's sad stories too. Friends, acquaintances and even total strangers would tell me their tragic story about how they had lost a partner, parent or sibling too soon in life and strangely, I really didn't mind hearing these devastating stories. I actually wanted to hear other people's bad news as it made me realise I wasn't alone in having a shit thing happen to. It was also very welcoming that people were talking to me about it and not skirting around the subject in fear of making me cry.

I felt like I was now in a club, a club of people that had lost someone close, a gang of grievers. An exclusive club that no one really wants to be a member of, but a club you have no choice about being initiated into. And there are few to no perks in being a member of this club also. A club where, if we all had membership cards with our sad story statistics on, it would be like playing an emotional and undesirable game of Top Trumps when we got together.

A friend of mine lost her long-term boyfriend three years after I lost Pete, so I was able to welcome her into this special club with her own Top Trump membership card. We both had level points in the death-timing category, as both our respective partners died suddenly and unexpectedly. However, I beat her in the marriage and kids category, as they didn't have any kids or weren't married yet, but she did beat me on the how-you-found-out category. She had the dreaded knock on the door from the police, whom she saw coming as she was looking out of the window due to her boyfriend being late home for dinner. After being informed of his accident, she was taken to the hospital for an agonising wait to then be told he had died.

In another Top Trump category, death location, her boyfriend died within a mile of where they lived and Pete died over 25 miles away. We score the same in this one because we both feel like the other one dipped out. She is glad it was close, so she doesn't have to travel far to visit the site, and I feel glad it's not close, so I don't have to pass the site on a regular basis, therefore a difficult category to score.

One thing not to say to someone grieving, especially at the funeral of a beloved boyfriend or girlfriend is, "Don't worry, there's plenty more fish in the sea!" which is what this friend had told to her whilst waiting in the queue for food at her boyfriend's wake. She definitely beats me in that Top Trump category of inappropriate comments made.

What I have learnt over the past eleven years is that there is no time limit or deadline for feelings. And you shouldn't feel like you should have to have one either. Yes, time is a great healer, the best healer, in fact, but we don't have a lot of time on this earth. Life does go on, no matter how much you don't want it to at times and that old saying, 'time is a great healer' will make you want to punch the person saying it to you in the face and kick them in a place you know will hurt, but time is the best healer there is. This book is about Pete and my journey coping and surviving his death, but no one person is the same and no one's life journey is the same either.

It's like pregnancy, for example. Not one birth is the same as another but for some reason, people love telling you their horror story of their child's birth, but this really is the last thing you want to hear. Especially when you have the impending doom of whatever is already trying to kick and punch its way out of your overstretched belly and making its way through some miracle transition onto the outside of your belly.

And like giving birth, sometimes the thought of something bad happening to you can actually be worse than the event itself. When it happens to you, you have no choice but to deal with it. It's happened, but the thought of it can be overwhelming. I had lots of people say to me, "I don't know what I'd do if I lost my husband/partner," or "I can't imagine what it must be like." Well, I didn't worry about Pete on that bike, maybe I should have, knowing his track record for hurting himself but either way, it was going to happen whether I worried or not.

Chapter Thirteen

One of the many other things I have learnt since Pete died is clichés are annoyingly truthful. For example, the one I've already mentioned about time being a great healer. At the time of Pete's death, this was the one thing I really didn't want to hear. I didn't want the pain I was feeling to last any length of time at all, I wanted to heal quickly with no fuss, but you can't heal quickly when something as life changing as that happens to you. You need time to go through all the emotions available, time to rebuild your life and time to repair your broken heart. Time is the only thing that can allow you to do that. Therefore, time is a great healer.

What doesn't kill you makes you stronger is a pretty self-explanatory one, but an absolutely truthful one too. There were plenty of times when I didn't know if I could carry on with life or if I even wanted to carry on without Pete, which made me feel very, very weak. There's no rulebook telling you how you should or shouldn't feel or any deadlines for when you should be 'getting over it' or when you should be feeling better and stronger. There were also times when I didn't think I would ever be able to stop crying, but I did and because of Pete's death and the aftermath I had to deal with, I am like an ice queen inside now, barriers firmly in place and I do feel that I can face anything emotionally distressing life has to throw at me and I will still survive!

Don't judge a book by its cover. Most of us are not mind readers and humans are pretty good at putting on a brave face whilst internally feeling like a crumbling mess, so don't presume that someone is happy and their life isn't in turmoil just because they are out in public and smiling. Also, common sense can become slightly clouded when trying to deal with someone who is grieving and people tend to not wear a badge informing you that they are trying to deal with some life or death issues so the first rule is, be nice to people. You don't know what that person is trying to deal with or has had to deal with in the past, so really, just be nice. Or if you can't be nice, just don't be a dick.

The elephant in the room. A really big rule in dealing with a grieving person is DO mention it! I know it's hard to know what to say to a person who has just lost someone through death and you really don't want to make that person cry or upset, but treating it like the elephant in the room will only make them feel like you don't care, which will make them feel a lot worse. All you need to do is say, "I'm so sorry to hear about (insert dead person's name), I'm thinking of you and sending you lots of love. If there is anything you need, just let me know." And try to say it without the obligatory head tilt or the trying-to-be-reassuring creepy arm touch. And don't be afraid to ask them how they are either, and don't panic if they do start crying. It's a natural process and when you're grieving, the fact that you're crying again in public will be a normal event and it really won't matter.

Life isn't a rehearsal, life is for living and there's no time like the present. When Pete died, it put a lot of things in my life into perspective. I was doing full-time mummy work, which I enjoyed most of the time, and part-time office work, which I hated most of the time. Whilst I was at work, I couldn't wait until home time and during the week, I couldn't wait for the weekend and of course, these times went so quickly that it was a neverending circle of wishing my life away.

And I was even more skint now, as Pete was the main breadwinner, so I decided life was for living and enjoying, therefore I needed a complete career change. I wanted a job that I liked or just didn't mind doing, and that might pay some good money. I had probably about 40 years left of my working life to endure at this point and because there's no time like the present and life's not a rehearsal, I went back to university to study a master's degree. Full time for five years whilst bringing up two young children with all of us still grieving. Sometimes you've just got to grab life by the balls and simply run with them in a firm grasp for as long as you can keep hold of them for.

Better safe than sorry. Although Dylan and Molly were my rocks many times along the way, I was their only parent, and I couldn't reassure them anymore that nothing would happen to me because they knew it possibly could and I would be lying if I said otherwise. I couldn't pull the smoke (excuse the pun) over their eyes anymore, and they gave me a massive guilt trip, which made me give up smoking because they told me they didn't want to lose another parent. Fair enough, really. But then I started to think about what I was doing in my life and would I now have to live an extremely boring life and do non-dangerous activities from now on, just in case. Not that I was into base jumping or crocodile wrestling, but it made me think about any consequences of my life choices for once and to be a bit safer rather than truly sorry.

The apple doesn't fall far from the tree. As heart breaking as it has been to see my kids grow up without a daddy, the most comforting thing for me has been having them around. Dylan looks just like his dad, has the same mannerisms and definitely the same warped sense of humour. Molly is very much like her dad in other ways. Worryingly, her clumsiness and lack of common sense, but also her intelligence and amazing ability to remember useful and useless facts. They are constant reminders of Pete, but they are nice reminders of Pete, so I am very glad that the apple didn't fall far from the tree after all.

Lightning never strikes twice in the same place or does it! One thing I have been unable to do since Pete's death is let the last thing I say to anyone be "have fun!" If those words exit my mouth, as I'm saying goodbye to them then I have to follow it up with "bye then" or "see you later" or "try not to die please!" I know I didn't cause Pete's accident by telling him to have fun before he left that day, but I'm really not taking any chances with this one.

Chapter Fourteen

Life goes on. Okay, so let's get all inspirational and talk about life now with some more added clichés. If you're reading this, then you're lucky to have a life to live. We only get one life, so make sure it's a life you want to live and do things that make you as happy as they can. Sometimes, we don't have a choice about the situations that life hands us and I strongly believe that you have to have some bad times to know what the good times are. Be thankful and grateful for things and try not to take them for granted. Pete was lucky enough to have 31 and a half years of life where he experienced growing up, having a job, hanging out with friends, having an amazing wife and two healthy and delightful kids, amongst many other things. A lot of people don't even get that long a life.

Every cloud has a silver lining. It can take time for the silver lining to be seen, but there will be one there if you search for it. Ruth said to me after Pete died that she was kind of jealous of Dylan and Molly, because at least they knew their daddy loved them. Her and Pete's dad, although still alive, did everything in his power not to see them or pay any maintenance money when they were growing, up giving the impression that he really didn't care about them, which makes me very sad. And because of him being an absolute arsewipe of a father, he has four gorgeous grandchildren he doesn't know; three of these he's never even met, he wasn't invited to two of the children's weddings, meaning he didn't give his eldest daughter away and he wasn't welcome, so he didn't attend the funeral of his eldest son. And we all won't attend his funeral either, so there is a couple of silver linings here. We all know there was a lot of love for and from Pete, and there is one less funeral we will all have to attend when Pete's dad dies.

Life, it is what it is and we are all dealt certain cards that we have no option but to take. It's not what happens to you, it's how you deal with it that will shape your future. What we think, we feel, so changing your mindset can make a massive difference to the way we feel about life. If you always think negative things or worry about stuff then that's going to make you feel anxious, unlucky, hard done by and depressed. If we change those thoughts and think 'fuck it, it's happened and worrying about it isn't going to change it' when bad things happen to us, we can turn that shit around. The mind is a very powerful thing, so do something that makes you happy like watch your favourite film, listen to your favourite music and dance like you just don't care, chat to your friends or just do anything you enjoy. This will make you feel better, which in turn will make you think about life in a much more enjoyable, positive and improved way.

The way I like to look at what happened to me is that when Pete died, my life got smashed into a billions pieces. After that, I had to build my life back up again, piece-by-piece, taking little baby steps all the way. Like building a wall back up, you place brick by brick by brick until you have a complete wall. Sometimes, things happen along the way and the pieces you've built up again get another knock back and sometimes, you don't feel like building those pieces back up at all but you have to. You have to keep slowly moving forward and keep building that wall of life back up again. And you can build it however you want, it's your wall of life and you are the only person responsible for building it.

Life is a double-edged sword. It took a while and a few knock backs along the way but I managed rebuild my wall of life back up again with the help from friends and family, and life after Pete has been really quite good. I now have a degree, I now have the prefix 'doctor' in front of my name, I now enjoy my job, I have two grown up unbelievably awesome kids and I am really bloody happy. Don't get me wrong, I still have bad days, I still miss Pete so much and I really wish he had never died. And although I love my job, I still do look forward to when I'm not working, but most of my life since Pete's death has actually been amazing.

Pete dying was a massively shit thing to happen, but if he hadn't died, then I'm not sure I'd be this happy today. I certainly wouldn't have gone back to study, therefore, I'd probably still hate my job and I'd still have a husband who irritated me regularly. Yes, it makes me feel very guilty about saying this, but life certainly is a doubled-edged sword. When life gives you lemons, make lemonade or better still, make a gin and tonic. And make that a double.

There's no time like the present so don't miss the boat. If you're not happy with an aspect of your life then change it. You're the only person that can so start today by making those baby steps towards your happiness. When you smile, the whole world smiles with you. When you cry, you cry alone. Unless, of course, you're at a funeral or watching *Watership Down*.

Chapter Fifteen

Laughter is the best medicine. Pete has been gone longer than I knew him for now, so I feel like the table of grief has turned for me and I feel as repaired as I'm ever going to be. The only thing that really makes me emotional these days is knowing that my children have had to grow up without their dad in their lives, and that will never go away for them. My heart breaks for them, it really does, and I still am and always will be there for them whenever they need me. Even when they tell me their dead-dad-jokes they have made up along the way. Whenever someone mentions a big car or a people carrier, Molly will plainly say "just like the one that killed my father", or pipe up with "must be nice to have a dad" when any one of her friends mentions their dad. Luckily, her friends have gotten used to her warped sense of humour now and I totally blame Pete for it.

Dylan's best dad joke came out of his mouth last Christmas. We went out to a local pub for our Christmas lunch, but there was a massive cock up by the pub and the food served to us was burnt and inedible. Dylan made the complaint that his Christmas lunch was more cremated than his father. Luckily, not in the earshot of the waiter, so I took that opportunity to remind Dylan that not everyone will find his extremely dark sense of humour as funny as we do.

So, in a nutshell, life can really suck, but life can also be bloody amazing too. Death really, truly sucks, but it may be absolutely awesome too. We don't know what awaits us on the other side. Don't sweat the small stuff in life, it isn't going to kill you, but if you let it consume you, it will make your life not so good. Money, you can't take it with you and money does not make you happy. Well, okay, so it does make me happier and it certainly makes life easier, but money alone will not complete your life. There are plenty of unhappy millionaires out there.

Have no regrets and remember, it's okay to cry and it's okay to smile. It's okay to be happy and it's okay to be sad. It's okay to feel guilty and it's okay to be selfish sometimes. It's okay to want to be alone and it's okay to need company. You have to make yourself your number one priority because no one else will make you their number one priority. And you are the only one who knows what you want. Life is too short and you never know what's round the corner or when your days are numbered. If you did know you were going to die tomorrow, what would you do?

One thing that will make me happy is knowing that after reading this book, you should be able to pronounce my fucking surname correctly!